60 One-Minute
Family Builders

Other Books by Dave and Claudia Arp

Beating the Winter Blues by Claudia Arp. This survival handbook for moms shows how to chase away the winter blues with 170 ways to have fun times and build family relationships.

52 Dates for You and Your Mate by Dave and Claudia Arp. A self-help book, containing 52 fun-packed dates to boost husband-wife communication.

Sanity in the Summertime by Claudia Arp and Linda Dillow. A survival guide for mothers to build strong relationships with their children in the summer and all year long.

The Marriage Track by Dave and Claudia Arp. Helps couples strengthen and build their marriage relationship using truths the authors have discovered from and share in their "Marriage Alive" workshops.

60 One-Minute Family Builders

Dave and Claudia Arp

Thomas Nelson Publishers
Nashville

Published in Nashville, Tennessee, by Thomas Nelson, Inc.

ISBN: 0-8407-4136-7

Printed in the United States of America.
1 2 3 4 5 6 7 8 9 10 11 12 13 14 15 16 17 18 19 20 — 98 97 96 95 94 93

To our parents,
Catherine and Joel Stembridge
and Lillian and David Arp,
for taking the time
to build into our lives.

C O N T E N T S

ACKNOWLEDGMENTS

Any attempt to list all who gave input would be incomplete. However, we especially want to acknowledge and express appreciation to the following:

Thanks to David and Vera Mace, who have been wonderful teachers and mentors and have modeled to us what a growing and healthy marriage looks like!

Thanks to the Association of Couples in Marriage Enrichment, founded by the Maces, and the ACME monthly publication that gave seed for many of our Minute-Builders. (For information about ACME write to P.O. Box 10596, Winston-Salem, NC 27108.)

Thanks to Paul and Leslie Lewis and their publication *Dad's Only* that has over the years fed good ideas for family fun to us and now on to our readers. (For information about *Dad's Only* write to P.O. Box 340, Julian, CA 92036.)

Thanks to Lynne Attaway for her expertise and help in editing this series.

And thanks to our three sons, Jarrett, Joel and Jonathan for being our human "guinea pigs" and allowing us to share our family memories with you.

INTRODUCTION

When is an ideal time to do fun, creative activities with our children? To many of us it might seem to be . . .

- when it's not raining and not too hot outside
- when we've had ten hours of sleep the night before
- when that big project at the office is finally completed
- when the phone isn't ringing
- when no one has a runny nose, a dirty bottom, or an upset stomach
- when our older children aren't at another activity and are actually home
- when we have a big block of time and we don't know how to fill it.

Our list could go on and on, but you get the picture! When is an ideal time to build relationships with our children? We would have to conclude—Never! It's not that we plan to neglect building family relationships, but in today's fast-paced world, it can easily happen. We can have good intentions and simply lack the time to carry them out. Some make the mistake of only looking for large blocks of time to do special things with their children. In a two-week summer vacation, they attempt to saturate each child with enough memories to last another year. They are determined to have fun and build memories, no matter how much pain and suffering it entails.

We remember some of our family vacations—some were more special than others. While we were living in Europe, we had a wonderful family vacation in Norway, and we still remember eating fresh shrimp in the rain in Oslo. But there are other vacations we'd like to forget—like the camping trip in the rain which, by the way, was our last family camping trip. Special family vacations are fine, but the relationships with our three sons were built more through the many things we did in the little minutes and moments of the dailies—our ten-minute chats, candlelight breakfasts, laughing together at Dad's sour humor (our boy's name for Dave's spontaneous and sometimes not-so-funny jokes).

Since our three boys were born within five years, it was good we could laugh together! Life wasn't always funny at the Arps'. We remember a toddler decorating a wall with his favorite colors of crayons and preschoolers throwing rocks at cars. In the elementary years they graduated to water balloons. We remember giving trust over and over again to our teens when they blew it and times when we realized that we, as parents, had blown it too.

The problem with being a parent is that by the time we are qualified, we're also unemployed. None of us are perfect parents. Dr. Howard Hendricks says that it's okay to make mistakes as long as we are willing to be honest with our children. Face it: they live with us; they already know we're not perfect! The good news is that we don't always have to be so serious or wear the perfect parent mask.

We've decided that at our house, we would rather err on the side of being too open and honest with our children, apologizing too much, laughing and having too much fun, concentrating too much on the relationships, than on the side of being too serious, too sober, and too sad. We wanted to enjoy parenthood while we lived through it.

If you too want to enjoy the parenting process, then our advice is to concentrate on building relationships with your children—and that's where our family-builders can help.

Building your family doesn't always require a big block of time, but it does require some time. Because we all have some time—however little—and because it's not always easy to know how to use it to build our families, we've put together this collection of minute family-builders to help you use the time you do have to build positive relationships with your kids.

Please don't try to master all the principles in this book in one week—you'll end up hating us and your family! Instead, we suggest that you use this book once a week or twice a month. It's not a book to read straight through, but instead is a resource of simple, easy, and quick ideas to help you build strong family relationships.

So whether you're a mom, dad, couple, single parent, guardian, grandparent—whatever your situation—let us encourage you to build the relationships with your children. Use the minutes you have now, for quickly, so quickly, the minutes, months, and years slip away. Before you know it, you, like us, will be looking at family life from the other end of parenting. What will you see? If you invest your minutes now, not only will you have healthy relationships with your adult children, but you will also influence future generations. Our world is counting on it!

PART ONE

APPETIZERS

HOME AND HUMOR

Is your home a fun place to be? Too often homes become tense. We take ourselves too seriously. How can we loosen things up a bit and turn our homes into fun places to be?

Don't be discouraged if laughter and fun don't exactly describe the atmosphere at your house. Some of us find it easy to joke and laugh. Others of us have to work at it.

Recently a successful businessman told us, "I can be light-hearted and joking with others, but when I get home I seem to tense up and take things too seriously." Here are some suggestions to add a little laughter to our homes.

1. Spend some time looking through old scrapbooks and pictures. We recently pulled out our college yearbooks and our wedding pictures. The boys chuckled when they saw their mom as a college majorette.

2. Go see a funny movie together or read a funny book. Cut out cartoons from the paper and put them on the refrigerator door.

3. Play with your kids—games that they want to play. Don't be ashamed to play softball even if you can't hit the ball. The game will be even funnier to them.

4. Be vulnerable to your kids—talk about the silly things you've done. Learn to laugh at yourself. Did something funny happen to you today? Then share it! You'll find you can learn to enjoy your family. Your home can be fun. And that's no laughing matter!

NEED A REBELLION PREVENTER?

Someone wisely said, "When it comes to raising kids, rules without a relationship lead to rebellion." How can we build a relationship with our children while maintaining those necessary rules?

Often in our desire to be good parents, we concentrate on consistently maintaining the rules, and we neglect building the relationship. However, maintaining the rules doesn't make us popular with our offspring. How can we reach a balance in this area? It's a continuous struggle for us, but here are a few ideas that have helped us.

1. We've found that we need to major on the majors and minor on the minors. We can't concentrate on everything, so in the important areas—like moral issues—we remain as steady as the Rock of Gibraltar. In the minor areas, we try to be flexible.

2. Communication is a two-way street. We try to really listen to our boys.

3. We are willing to say, "I was wrong." If you're like us, you may find that sometimes the teen is right and you are wrong. Don't be too proud to say, "Hey, I was wrong. Please forgive me."

4. Do things together with the kids. Remember those special one-to-one times. Relationships are built in twos. What can you do today to build that special relationship?

Remember, your relationship can be a rebellion preventer in your home!

TV OR DAD?

Four- and five-year-olds in a Michigan State University study, when offered a hypothetical choice of whether to give up TV or give up their father, voted three-to-one to give up dad! How would your kid vote? Let's take a look at our competition—that one-eyed monster called the television—and get it working for us, not against us.

Here are some suggestions to get you started.

1. Let younger children *earn* TV viewing time by trading it for equal time spent reading, doing chores or homework, or practicing skills. Set up a chart to record time.

2. Charge ten cents for thirty minutes of TV viewing. Put the money in a bank on the top of the TV and save it for a special family outing.

3. Plan ahead. Choose a good family program like the Bill Cosby show. Watch it together; then discuss what you saw.

4. At football time, have your own tailgate party. Why not pop corn, put down a blanket, and have a *ball* right in your own den?

With a little preplanning, TV can be a friend to your family togetherness. You can make it work for you!

LEARNING TO SAY NO

D o you have a difficult time saying the word *No?* If saying no is as hard for you as it is for us, then you may also need help in using that little, but important, word. It's especially difficult when we have to say no to perfectly good things.

Pat King's book *How to Have All the Energy You Need Every Day* gives us some good suggestions for saying no. Check out these different kinds of no's.

- There's the perfectly valid no: "I've been out three nights this week. I'm staying home to-night and spending time with my family." Say it as if you mean it!

- Then there's the no after you have said yes: "No, I've made a mistake. I shouldn't have committed myself. I'm sorry. I'll have to back out." Then hang up the phone and give a huge sigh of relief.

- How about the five-star no (This is our favorite . . . there's no comeback for it.): "I'll have to pass it up."

- We like this one. It's the not-right-now no: "I've done it in the past and I'll do it in the future, but I can't do it now."

- For a polite no, say: "I'm sorry, but my schedule doesn't permit me to take on any more obligations this week." You could also use month or year, whatever is appropriate!

- Along with the polite no is the diplomatic no: "It was so kind of you to think of me. I'm flattered you asked. I'm sorry I won't be able to do it."

- If all else fails, you can use the absolute no: "I cannot do this. I don't have the desire, the time, the interest, or the energy. NO! Absolutely not ever!"

Take it from us, practice saying no more often and you'll find you do have the time and energy you need for an important "Yes" when the opportunity enters your life!

SURPRISES ADD SPICE

What describes the routine in your home? Unpredictable or variable or humdrum? With children in your home, you probably don't have a dull routine, but can your children predict you?

Would you like to break out of a humdrum routine and add to the unexpected? Family relations can be refreshed and stimulated by adding an element of surprise.

Surprises can make tough times easier to bear—especially as you remind yourself that up ahead there may be a totally unexpected turn of events.

So how can you surprise your family? Here are a few suggestions:

1. Fill someone's closet with balloons. Write a note on each one.

2. Kidnap your mate or your child, and take him or her out for a special treat.

3. Throw a party for some normally unheralded event like the dog's birthday or the first snowfall.

4. Do something out of character: Wear a fake nose to the dinner table or leave notes in the refrigerator.

5. Why not switch places at the dinner table tonight? Each person can try to act like the person who usually sits in that place.

When we do the unexpected, it adds to our family fun. One time Dave went by the high school and switched cars with one of our sons. Imagine his surprise when he ran out after school and found the family station wagon had been upgraded—he had our nicest car to drive home. It changed his perspective for the whole day.

Surprise your family today, and wipe out boredom in your home.

DINNER RESEARCH

What do you think goes on at the dinner table of a typical American family? This question was the subject of a three-year survey done by the Educational Testing Service of Princeton, New Jersey. Families were videotaped in their homes at regular meals.

If the researchers came to dinner at your house, what would they find? Here are some results from their survey.

In small families, the conversation is active among parents and children. But as family size grows, parents spend more time controlling the children, and there is less real conversation.

The middle children suffer the most since the parents talk more with the older children or spend time helping the younger ones. The biggest offense at dinner is the television takeover, which deprives everyone in the family of attention.

That's really too bad since the survey showed that parents' questions can stimulate a rise in children's IQs. Conversation, rather than TV observation, is caring, sharing, joyful, and educational. So if you have a TV, you might let it live in another room than the one where you eat!

On the brighter side, the survey showed that some families are returning to the old-fashioned dinner at the table. They read a chapter of a book at the dinner table, or they talk about the day's events and world news and enjoy the warmth of being together.

At such homes, food may be the least important ingredient of the evening meal . . . what about at yours? Think about it!

TIPS FOR
TALKING WITH TEENS

Do you ever have a problem talking with your teens? One dad said, "Sure I do. How do you talk to a teen who lives in a cave and only comes out three times a day to eat and grunt at the family?"

Here are seven tips that could revolutionize parent-teen communication:

1. Express your desires and fears specifically. Teens need clear guidelines and boundaries, and they need to know how we feel. It's OK to say, "I get angry when you do that" or "I worry when you don't come home on time."

2. Don't bombard your teen with questions. No one likes to be cross-examined.

3. Don't beg. If you do, you give away power, and it's just not worth it. Besides, begging is not effective.

4. Negotiate boundaries, but do it from a position of strength. You are the parents, and some decisions must be yours—not all, but some.

5. Don't be intimidated by a teen's attempt to create guilt feelings. Remember, your value as a person does not depend on how your teen performs or behaves.

6. Relax and slow down. If you're under stress from a situation that doesn't involve your teen, don't let that tension spill over onto him or her. Look for the humor in a situation, and try not to take life so seriously.

7. Don't be afraid to share your childhood with your teen. One good way to get information from your teenager is to share yourself—especially your own fears, uncertainties, and difficulties as an adolescent.

When our teens see that we are real and don't claim to be perfect, then they are free to open up and talk. Don't forget to listen—you're in for a real treat.

You may be amazed at the great person your teen has become—but it's not really so amazing. Just look at the family background!

CHILDREN AND STRESS

Is your child suffering from chronic stress? In the high-pressure, fast-paced society we live in, it's easy for our children to suffer from stress. Are you aware of any signs of stress in your children?

Psychologist Carl Thoresen, a Stanford University researcher, reports that one of every five American high-school students shows signs of chronic stress. The cause? Among the reasons given were high-pressure parents and a fast-paced society.

Kids suffering from chronic stress often exhibit competitiveness and impatience. They tend to internalize anger and seem less confident than other kids.

Other symptoms of stress include sweaty palms, rapid heartbeat, muscle tension, and sleeping trouble. Although this research project was done on children at the high-school level, Thoresen says there's every reason to believe that stress may be prevalent among elementary-school children.

A fast-paced competitive society probably contributes to stress. But parents who pressure children to achieve could also be a cause. One father participating in a research project gave more than one hundred directions to his child in eight minutes.

Now is a good time to stop and consider these questions:

1. Is my child showing symptoms of stress?

2. What might I be doing to add to his or her stress?

3. What could I do today to relieve stress in my home?

Think about it and act. You can be a stress reliever in your home!

NINE

TALK,
DON'T BUG

When you try to communicate with your teenager, are you a talker or a "bugger"? You may think you're talking when actually you're bugging. How can you tell the difference?

Once we asked Joel, "What tips do you have for parents who really want to communicate with their teens?" His answer was short and to the point. He said, "Talk, don't bug!"

Needing a little clarification, we asked him, "What's the difference?" He said, "Bugging is when you talk in order to get your kid to do something." We immediately felt guilty.

"Talking," he said, "is when you don't want anything and you communicate." That made us stop and evaluate how we were doing. Too often as parents we do have some goals we'd like to achieve when we talk to our teens, or we have some good advice to give. We'll communicate better if we save our advice for the family pet.

Here's a challenge for you and for us: For the next twenty-four hours, see how much talking you do without bugging. That means no advice or subtle manipulation.

Oh, we also asked Joel, "What's a parent to do when he needs to get a kid to do something?" His answer? "Bug 'em!" Maybe if we do a lot of talking, a little bugging is OK!

PART TWO

MAIN DISHES

TIME FOR COMMUNICATION

True or false? Most families have plenty of time to develop good habits and skills in family communication.

How we wish that statement were true. But it's not in our home. We have to work hard to find the time to invest in improving our communication. How about you?

It's easy to get busy and forget to take the time to really communicate. We get into bad habit patterns, and as you know, habits are hard to change.

In addition, we put off changes until tomorrow, and somehow tomorrow never arrives.

Often we say, "Next week won't be so busy. We'll talk about it then." But next week comes, and we still don't talk about it.

So today we challenge you to take the time to start to build a stronger home through better communication. You can change habits, but it does take work.

Psychologists tell us it takes three weeks to make a new habit and six weeks to feel good about it. For the next few weeks why not choose a Communication Rule of the Week?

Here are some suggestions to get you started.

Week One—Decide to stop using *why* questions. *Why* questions tend to be threatening. Ask questions, but phrase them differently.

Week Two—Use *I* statements instead of *you* statements. You'll find you're doing less attacking.

Week Three—Start sharing prayer requests as a family and praying together. We find breakfast is a good time for doing this in our family.

We hope our tips will be helpful to you. Remember, good communication is habit-forming. Why not get addicted today?

ELEVEN

HOW TO GET
A KID TO TALK

How do you get a kid to talk? Try an art that requires much practice. It's called listening! Listening is certainly one of the most important skills of parenting. How can we as parents become better listeners? When parents listen with interest, children feel that their ideas are valued and that they are respected. This gives the child a sense of self-esteem and confidence as the child reasons, "If my parents believe I'm worth listening to, I must be a person of value and importance."

Here are four tips to help you be a better listener.

1. Be attentive. Stop what you're doing as soon as you can and give full attention. Remember the importance of eye contact. Be sensitive to the tone of voice and facial expression.

2. Encourage talk. Smiles, nods, and one-word responses indicate interest. Keep questions

brief, open, and friendly, and try to avoid asking *why* questions.

3. Empathize with your child. Try to put yourself into his or her shoes. Now this may take imagination and patience, but it will help you understand your child's actions and reactions much better.

4. Listen with respect. Try to react to your child as you would to an adult friend. Listen as much as you talk. And face the fact that at times kids are complainers. Let them get their grievances off their chests.

Learning to listen can help to build closeness with our children. It also can help young people release pent-up emotions. Our listening can strengthen their ability to make decisions and solve their own problems.

The art of listening may require much practice, but it's one art that will greatly help you to build relationships in your home. Now, did you hear that?

FORGIVENESS IS VITAL

Love means never having to say you're sorry, except about ten times a week when you're wrong, bullheaded, inconsiderate, forgetful, stupid, or lazy! Get the picture? Let's look at how to say, "I blew it. I'm sorry."

We have five independent thinkers in our family. When we are all together, it's easy to overreact. We've found that love is being willing to say, "Hey, I blew it again, and I'm sorry!"

Here are a couple of tips for saying you're sorry in the right way:

1. When you blow it and have to apologize, let the statement reflect back on you and avoid attacking the other person. Say, "I'm sorry I overreacted, will you forgive me?" instead of saying, "You made me overreact, but I'm sorry anyway."

2. Avoid justifying yourself. Don't say, "I'm sorry I overreacted, but you would too if you were as tired as I am."

To show love in your home, take the initiative. Be the first to say, "I'm sorry." With a little practice, you'll find it's not too hard at all, and your family will be stronger for it!

HOW TO LOVE A TEENAGER

Are you looking for ways to really love your teenager? Those unique creatures called teenagers are sometimes easy to love; at other times—well, maybe you, too, need some suggestions.

Here are some ways to get started:

1. Do things together—biking, backpacking, tennis, Frisbee, shopping, or anything else your teenager likes to do.

2. Attend important events like school athletic games, plays, and open houses.

3. With enthusiasm, teach him or her to drive.

4. Help your teen find an enjoyable job.

5. Provide transportation with joy and without complaint.

Before you know it, that son or daughter will have his or her driver's license. Gone will be many of the great times you can have right now while you drive here and there.

6. Listen to his or her favorite music and receptively discuss it.

7. Make an honest effort to get to know his or her friends. Have an open home policy. If the gang is ganging up at your house, you will know where your teen is.

8. Read a book or magazine your teen is reading.

9. Give generously of your time, presence, and emotional energy. It may be one of the best investments you'll ever make!

PARENTAL BEHAVIOR

Are your children pleased with your behavior as a parent? So often we concentrate on our children's behavior and not our own! Let's stop and take a look at parental behavior from the child's perspective.

Consider the results of a survey of 100,000 children ages eight through fourteen from twenty-four countries. The children were asked what they wanted most in their parents.

Check out the top ten. They want:

1. Parents who don't argue in front of them.

2. Parents who treat each family member the same.

3. Parents who are honest.

4. Parents who are tolerant of others.

5. Parents who welcome their friends to the home.

6. Parents who build a team spirit with their children.

7. Parents who answer their questions.

8. Parents who give punishment when needed, but not in front of others, especially their friends.

9. Parents who concentrate on good points instead of weaknesses.

10. Parents who are consistent.

How do you rate? We hope you've picked up some tips that keep you from being a behavior problem to your children!

PARENTAL PEER PRESSURE

Are you a victim of parental peer pressure? We hear a lot about teenage peer pressure, but what about us as parents? Are you being pressured by your peers?

Peer pressure is not unique to young people. We're all influenced by others. If you don't believe it, just check out your closet. When we base important decisions about our family on what others would say or think, we get into dangerous waters.

Sometimes we just don't think, and we go along with the flow. We say yes or no because other parents have gone in that direction. It may be the right decision; the other parents may be correct. But the guiding principle shouldn't be to do what others think is right or what others have done.

We try to evaluate things from another perspective. Here are some questions we use in our family:

1. Is it a moral issue? If it is, it's a major, and parental peer pressure goes out the window.

2. Are there guiding Biblical principles to follow? These also are not negotiable.

3. Another important question is how will it effect our family and what's best for our child?

If it endangers us or our child, then forget what other parents may say or do.

The answers to these three questions help to give a clearer picture of what we are dealing with and which issues are involved. Maybe these questions will help you to resist becoming a victim of parental peer pressure. Why not try them and see for yourself?

STRONG-WILLED CHILDREN

Is your family blessed with a strong-willed child? "Strong-willed?" asked one parent. "Why, my daughter gave the term strong-willed a whole new meaning. It's not that she's inflexible; she's totally brittle." Perhaps you can identify with this parent.

While some children seem to be born with an easygoing, compliant attitude toward life, others seem to be defiant from the time they are born. Dr. James Dobson, in his excellent book, *The Strong-Willed Child*, offers good advice to parents.

According to Dr. Dobson, an understanding that the defiant child is a rather common character—and not necessarily the product of poor discipline—should give some comfort to those parents who face the challenge of shaping such a strong will.

He gives six guidelines for dealing with a strong-willed child:

1. Distinguish between willful defiance and childish irresponsibility. When children forget to

feed the dog or carelessly lose a sweater, remember that these immature behaviors are typical of childhood.

2. Define the boundaries before you enforce them.

3. When your child defiantly challenges you, respond with confident decisiveness. When a parent says, "Don't," and the child looks him or her in the eye and does it anyway, that's defiance. It is extremely important for the adult to be firm and back up the command with discipline. The discipline may be time out or loss of privileges or some other method. The child must know that if he defies a rule, he will pay the consequences.

4. Reassure and teach after the confrontation is over. Immediately after the conflict, hold the child close and verbally reaffirm your love.

5. Avoid impossible demands. Sometimes we expect our child to be more mature or perfect than we are.

6. Let love be your guide. Dobson reminds us that rules without a relationship lead to rebellion. But a warm relationship characterized by genuine love and affection is likely to be healthy even if the parents make mistakes.

Take Dr. Dobson's advice. It will help you avoid guilt and anxiety as you raise your strong-willed child.

ELIMINATING TRUSTBUSTERS

Has your child really "blown it?" Do you feel you just can't trust him or her any more? Well, you may think, "It's my child who's the trust-buster in this family," but we want to challenge you to reexamine your ideas about trust.

Listen to what Fritz Redenour says, in his book, *What Teenagers Wish Their Parents Knew About Kids*.

"You might as well trust your teenager; you don't have any other reasonable choice. Distrust simply breeds more distrust, but if you keep trusting your teenager, sooner or later the message will get through."

Even though your child has made a major mistake, you as the parent need to keep trusting that child. You can avoid these trustbusters.

1.   "If I can't trust you in this area, how can I trust you in other areas?" Trust is not a one-time gift. It must be given time and time again. Too often when a teenager is irresponsible in one

area, the parent generalizes from one mistake to everything else the teen does—like the parent who said, "You broke your curfew again, so I can't trust you to be responsible in your schoolwork! You must come directly home after school and study for two hours each day!"

2. "Earn our trust, and then we'll trust you." How can your child prove he or she is trustworthy without being given some freedom to make decisions? Soon after Joel got his driver's license, we let him drive to work. One morning Dave found his books strewn all over the trunk of the car. Joel had been doing figure-eights in the parking lot where he worked. He received a stern lecture, but we allowed him to continue to drive to work. Why? We wanted to give him the opportunity to be more careful in the future.

Remember, eliminate parent trustbusters and give your child the gift of trust.

PART THREE

TIME-FINDERS

GIVING FOCUSED ATTENTION

Do you focus on "focused attention" in your home? We all need that one-to-one time with those we love.

L. Ross Campbell, in *How To Really Love Your Child*, defines focused attention this way: "Focused attention is giving a child our full, undivided attention in such a way that he feels without a doubt that he is completely loved. That he is valuable enough in his own right to warrant his parents' undistracted watchfulness, appreciation and uncompromising regard."

In short, focused attention makes a child feel he is the most important person in the world in his parents' eyes. How can we give focused attention to those special people in our lives?

Focused attention requires time—sometimes lots of it. Here are some ways you can find that time to give your children focused attention.

1. When a younger child is napping, take time with the older.

2. When a brother or sister is at a friend's house, spend time with one of the other children.

3. When an older child is at an activity, entertain the younger one at home.

4. Hire a babysitter for one, two, or more children, and go someplace with one child.

5. Trade off children with friends so that you can spend time alone with one.

Small children need smaller blocks of time alone with one parent while with older kids and teens . . . well, you just have to wing it. Our teenagers didn't get excited about preplanned Just-Me-and-Mom/Dad Times, but they did enjoy time alone—when it just happened.

It won't be easy, but hang in there. Both you and your children will be the winner as Just-Me-and-You Times become a tradition at your house!

NINETEEN

A DISEASE IS THREATENING YOUR FAMILY!

What if we told you a disease was killing your entire family? Certainly the shock would cause you to launch a frantic search for the cure. Actually, there is a disease that is threatening your family life, the disease of overcommitment. If your family is typical, overcommitment has been eating away at the insides of your marriage and family relationships for years. We realized life at the Arps' was too hectic when the oven went out one Sunday and no one missed it until the next Sunday.

Frequently overcommitment isn't discovered until it's too late. Here are some symptoms you may be noticing:

You've said yes to so many fine activities, even for the kids, that you scatter in every direction. Even if you do use your oven and cook dinner, no one is home to eat it.

Or maybe you've said yes to so many purchases that you have to work too hard to pay the bills. Why is it so hard to learn that possessions don't build strong families?

47

You've said yes to so many hours of television that you've been robbed of those family vitamins called talking and reading together.

We are sad to report that the National Center for Disease Control is not presently studying this epidemic called overcommitment, but we do have some good news for you if you are a victim.

The cure is free and has been known to us for centuries. It's an uninviting capsule full of time-released pellets you must take daily. Each pellet is shaped like the word "No."

Take a couple of minutes and make a list of things you should and can say no to. Try it—it'll be good for your family's health!

ALTERNATIVES TO TV

Would you like to break the TV habit or at least reduce the addiction? Then stop and think about what isn't on television! Now we're not debating the pros and cons of TV viewing. We have our favorite programs, but if all we do as a family is watch the tube, we're in big trouble.

Consider these family entertainment alternatives:

1. Read together as a family. C. S. Lewis' Narnia series is great reading for families with early-elementary-age children.

2. Listen to the radio. Stations like your National Public Radio station carry good family programs in the late afternoon or early evening. Pop some corn and gather around the way your grandparents used to do, listening to a good program. Then discuss what you heard.

3. Visit an art gallery. Make it an outing for the whole family. Cap it off with a snack or beverage while you talk about what you saw—what you liked and what you didn't.

4. Attend a live drama. Even a high school or other amateur production can be entertaining. Check with local schools for upcoming events.

5. Attend a concert. Many local orchestras also have free outdoor concerts. Invest in tickets to the symphony.

6. Check out local sports. Don't stop after you think of football. Consider other sports too, like soccer, hockey, track and field, tennis. The list could go on and on.

7. A final suggestion: have friends over. Instead of TV viewing, you could play board games, have a sing-along, hold a storytelling competition. You may discover that some of the best entertainment isn't on TV. You may even find that you are your own best entertainment!

FIVE-YEAR-OLDS AND DIRTY SOAP

You can always tell a home with a five-year-old in it. You have to wash the soap before you use it! Perhaps you're in that special stage of family life when you have more dirty soap than time. Finding time for family when life is spelled h-e-c-t-i-c is not always easy. Here's a tip. Look for time you can use twice.

Think about travel time. You can fill this time with conversation, games, and songs. You already have a captive audience.

What about mealtimes? Why not make an agenda box? Let family members put in anything they would like the family to talk about. Be creative and adapt this idea. You might prefer a riddle box or a joke box.

Bedtimes can be special times of closeness—time for stories, talks about hopes and fears, and prayer time together.

One clever dad created a "morning college." While he shaves each morning, his kids can ask any question they can think of, and he has to do his best to answer.

How much time does it take to talk to a five-year-old? As much as you can find. But you're certain to find more of it if you make the most of life's many small routine situations!

CELEBRATION TIMES

How long has it been since you've had a celebration at your house? Too often we wait for special events to come along like birthdays and official holidays, and then we're rushed. No wonder so many celebrations feel more like obligations. What can we do to change this and add some excitement to family life?

We don't have to wait for a big event—but we do have to slow down. Stop right now, and set aside some time today. Look at those special people and events that surround you. Think about the next few weeks, and see if you can discover some reason for celebrating.

Here are some ideas to pull off a family celebration.

1. Is there a significant milestone coming up? Perhaps a teen got that treasured driver's license or someone successfully completed a soccer league or a child learned to dress himself this week.

2. Consider a noteworthy accomplishment like a spouse's promotion, a music recital, or a football victory.

3. Remember anniversaries, like the anniversary of the morning the stray cat came to join your family or of your move into your present home.

4. You can celebrate the natural beauty of a sunset or the leaves changing color.

5. Celebrate when something comes to an end—like having braces removed or making the final car payment.

6. You can have a celebration for no reason at all. Help your family today to appreciate the good things and those worthy of our joy. Your family will appreciate it!

COMMUNICATION CENTER

Do you know where the communication center is in your house? Have you ever stopped and analyzed just where your kids open up and talk the most?

In other words, where is your home communication center? One thing's for sure—it's probably NOT where the home entertainment center is! TV tends to hinder, not help, communication in most families.

In our home we get into the best conversations in the den—especially in the winter when we build a fire. Sometimes we slip in there to have a few moments alone or relax, and before we know it the others start slipping in.

Maybe in your home it's on the screened porch or in a bedroom, or maybe it's in the kitchen. Our sons often come in the kitchen and talk when they smell something good baking in the oven.

We like the British tradition of tea time. Why not surprise your family with an unexpected sit-down snack? You could even be British and have tea.

To help get conversations going at your house, here's a tip for you. For the next couple of days watch your conversation places, and see where communication flows easily at your house. Then plan to hang around with your listening ear.

But a word to the wise: Leave advice, lectures, and value judgments in the other room. Practice listening. Your communication center is vital and can be the center of warmth in your home!

FINDING TIME IN LITTLE PLACES

Are you looking for more time for your family? You may find it in the little places. We've never met a person who complained of having too much time with their family, but we've talked to many who complain of having too little.

How can we find more time to invest in our family relationships? First, realize that everything doesn't have to be done immediately. Our minds work faster than our bodies. We get ahead of ourselves and fall behind before we start.

Second, realize that time comes in little places. For instance, when you turn off the TV, you find time. Putting the TV where it's less accessible may help.

Another place to find time is around the evening meal. Try eating in the dining room or someplace other than the kitchen. The pots and pans and general disarray won't grab your attention. We love to eat on our screened porch. It's a little place we find quality time as a family.

Remember time in the car together. Some of our best conversations with our boys have been as we have driven them to school and other activities.

Time isn't easy to find, but when we look in the little places, we may discover it's already there!

RAINBOWS

The work will wait while you look at the rainbow, but the rainbow won't wait while you do the work. Recently after a rain shower we saw a beautiful rainbow. How relaxing it was just to look up and see the lovely colors spread across the sky. There are other rainbows to enjoy as well—the kind we find right in our homes with our families.

Maybe you can identify with us. We're both goal-oriented and can get so involved in finishing the task and reaching our goals that we can easily miss the rainbows along the way.

Many parents get so involved in providing for and doing things for their children that they miss the simple rainbows:

1. Looking for a moment at a sleeping child.

2. Taking an extra couple of minutes to sit and laugh together when family communication is clicking.

3. Taking a cookie break. Don't just bake the cookies. Sit down and eat them together.

4. Stopping long enough to join in on a TV program or even listen to the children's music!

5. Saying, "Sure, I have time for a game of tennis."

6. Touring your yard or a local park and enjoying smelling the roses.

7. Checking the young plants in your vegetable garden and watching for the first tomato or zucchini.

Take a few minutes right now. Survey your family and home. You'll be amazed at all the beautiful rainbows you will find!

FAST-LANE
FAMILY STRESS

Is your fast-lane life getting out of control? It's easy in our culture to get too busy and find ourselves losing control. This certainly doesn't add to our family life. Here are some tips for taking the fast lane a little more slowly:

1. Do the most important things first. You might want to make a list of things you need to do and then number them by importance. If you don't get through your list, at least you have done the most important things. At the end of the day, transfer anything undone to a new list for tomorrow. Then you can tear up your old list. That always makes us feel good.

2. Group your related activities together. If you're out grocery shopping you might as well fill up the car with gas.

3. Divide big jobs into workable steps.

4. Use a timer to see how much you can accomplish in 15 minutes.

5. Do all you can to finish a job completely, but don't feel like a failure if you don't get everything finished.

6. To avoid fast-lane trauma, learn when to say no.

Don't get so busy that you can't smell the flowers along the way. Life is too enjoyable to hurry through it!

PART FOUR

FAMILY VITAMINS

IS YOUR HOUSE A HOME?

Webster's defines a house as a structure for human habitation, but it defines a home as the abiding place of the affections. How do you make your house a home? Start by recognizing that the atmosphere is a lot more important than the decor. What's the atmosphere like in your home?

We've found that one vital element in our home is laughter, not at each other but with each other. Laughter lightens any load and says nonverbally, "I'm enjoying being with you."

Mutual respect is also important. We consider our boys our friends as well as our sons. Why is it we sometimes forget to treat our families as important people? Many times it's easier to be courteous to a clerk or the bagger at the grocery store than it is to be kind to those special people in our homes.

To create a loving and warm atmosphere in your home remember to do the little things, like playing pleasant background music. When our boys were younger, we found that happy music in the background cut down on their fights.

Candlelight is an economical way to create a warm atmosphere, and there's nothing quite like the smell of cookies baking in the oven! But don't stop there; take the time to sit down with your family and eat them.

Remember, that house where you and your family live can be a real home. Determine today to make it a happy place, and it will be home to your family!

INDICATORS OF STRONG FAMILIES

What traits do you think would best describe strong families? Three thousand families from around the world recently participated in a program to reveal family strengths.

The results were presented at the 1985 Symposium on the Family at Pennsylvania State University. Here are the top six traits of strong families.

1. Strong families spend time doing things together. This includes work, play, and meals together—not easy to accomplish in today's world, but not impossible!

2. They were committed to one another. If one family member was in trouble, the other members gave their support, time, and energy. They did what they could to promote growth, happiness, and welfare of the others.

3. Family members talk a lot about both trivial and deep subjects. They do disagree, but they

work to find solutions on the issues that come up.

4. They have a high degree of religious orientation. God is involved in their day-to-day struggles, giving purpose, meaning, and the power to relate in the right way.

5. They deal with crisis in a positive way. They are one another's support system. Strong families see something positive in the crisis and focus on the positive rather than the negative.

6. They show lots of appreciation for each other. Just like miners who dig to find precious gems, they don't mind moving tons of dirt to find the diamond.

Why don't you check out your own family? You may find you are stronger than you think. You may even find lots of diamonds you didn't know you had!

HONESTY AND OPENNESS

Healthy homes have a generous dose of these two traits—honesty and openness. These two helpful words should be in the conscious vocabulary of every good parent. How can we make sure that "honesty" and "openness" describe our own family relationships?

Openness is basically the willingness to grow. The person who is open hates to get in a rut and is willing to try new things. How long has it been since your family did something new or different?

Why not try to do one new thing together this week? Maybe you'll want to get everyone up early one morning and go out for breakfast together before work and school.

Our other word is honesty. That's simply telling the truth with love and compassion. Too many times we don't express ourselves, and we keep our opinions to ourselves.

The most healthy families are those who emphasize separate identities, individual interests, and each person's uniqueness. To do that, families have to be open with one another.

But at the same time they work at building their family life together around their common interests and mutual tastes.

Check to see that each family member has a unique and individual interest. Now check to see that as a family you have some interest in common.

Take the time today to see that openness and honesty are words that describe the atmosphere in your family relationship. You'll benefit from it. And that's the honest truth!

GOOD LISTENING

Did you ever think about the fact that God gave us two ears and only one mouth? Maybe we're supposed to listen twice as much as we are to speak. How well do you listen to others? Let's look at an important part of the communication circuit —the input, better known as listening.

Here are some tips to help us keep our tongues still and our ears open from Alan Lay McGinnis's book, *The Friendship Factor.*

1. First, good listeners listen with their eyes. The eye lock is a powerful magnet for making contact with people. It's a clear sign that you're interested.

2. Second, good listeners give advice sparingly. Nothing cuts off communication quite like giving advice.

3. Good listeners never break a confidence. Trust is a tremendous gift. Handle with care by learning to zip your lip.

Remember, when you listen attentively to another person, you pay a high compliment. You show that you value what he or she is thinking. So make an effort today. Keep your incoming circuits available to those you love.

TAKE A PARENTING CHECKUP!

We get dental and physical checkups regularly. Why not a parenting checkup? Take a couple of minutes to evaluate how you're doing as a parent and ways in which you'd like to change or improve.

Here are five questions to help you do just that:

1. How am I spending time with my children? Is it quality time? Is it enough? You might stop to think through last week and add up the amount of time you actually spent with your children.

2. Do I have role models for my job as a parent? We always looked for families that we admired with children who were several years ahead of ours. Then we asked lots of questions and observed what they were doing.

3. Am I teaching my children the skills and attitudes they need for successful living?

4. What are my strengths as a parent? What areas do I really need to work on?

5. What are my most cherished memories so far with each of my children? What memories do I want to build before it's too late?

To consolidate your thoughts, write down your parental diagnosis. Then be practical and write out your prescription for spending time with your kids. Your whole family will benefit!

TIPS FOR FAMILIES WITH SICK KIDS

Have the sniffles, sneezes, and flu bugs invaded your home? If you're a typical family, sometime this year you'll probably answer yes.

What can you do when you have a homebound child? These times can be special. Here are some tips from our friends, the Dan Porters, to make the hours and days pass quickly.

1. To make your child feel special, keep a small bell at the child's bedside. Family members can take turns being on duty for the patient, answering the ring of the bell.

2. Make an official medical chart to record diet, medications, temperature, and other items of interest. You could also make a countdown calendar to keep track of the days until the child goes back to school or finishes the antibiotics.

3. Turn off the TV and play lots of games. Keep scorecards and have a family tournament.

4. Make a lap desk by using an empty packing box. Just cut a half-circle in the two long sides of the box and leave the ends as they are. It will fit nicely over your patient as he sits in the bed.

5. Cut out comic strips from newspapers and write your own funny lines, or let the child write his or her life history and illustrate it.

6. For a younger child, make a lifesize doll, using old toddler garments for clothing. This can be a comical bedmate for a sick child.

7. Realize that days home with a sick child will not be your most productive days. Your "to do" list will probably grow longer, not shorter. Relax and grab the opportunity to have that special one-to-one time.

Your love and pampering will be as valuable as any tonic or medication, and that's our prescription for a happy family on sick days.

PARENT-TEACHER CONFERENCES

How do you feel when the phone rings and it's your child's teacher asking you to come for a parent-teacher conference? Do you panic, worry, or just feel unprepared and a little apprehensive? We've certainly experienced all those emotions in our family. With fall days, school buses, and football games comes another aspect of school life—parent-teacher conferences. Let's look at how we can prepare and get the most out of them.

The first tip is to prepare for the meeting ahead of time. Check with your child to see if he or she has any concerns. Write down things you would like to discuss like classroom policies, your child's performance, or whatever concerns you.

Second, be willing to ask questions. Here's your chance to get the facts about any school situation that you only know secondhand. Be open in discussing your child's achievements, health, and activities. The teacher sees only one side of your child. You can help the teacher see your child in a positive way.

Third, explain about any special experiences or schooling your child has had. We always tried to let our boys' teachers know that they had basically grown up in Europe and studied in a completely different school system. This helped the teacher to understand if they were behind in an area.

We also stressed that our boys respond better to praise than to reprimand. We wanted to help the teacher see the potential that was yet to be developed.

Fourth, let the teacher know you want to help. One of your best investments in your children's lives is the time you spend being a volunteer in their schools.

So when that phone call comes from your child's teacher, you can respond positively, "Yes, I would love to come by for a visit."

PREVENTING MOVING TRAUMA

Is a move coming up for your family? If so, you can avoid moving trauma! If you're considering a move in the near future, whether you are moving to another town, another state, or just across the street, we have some tips to help you reduce moving trauma for your family. We've made four major moves. Two of them were to other countries, so we know firsthand what moving trauma is all about.

Recently we talked with a family whose four-year-old daughter was exhibiting classic symptoms of moving trauma—complete with "the whines." She had watched as all her toys were packed away in boxes and was afraid that she would never meet them again.

If a move is in your future, here are some tips that may help it go more smoothly, especially if you have young children:

1. Let each child choose one or two favorite toys to keep out of the packing boxes and person-

ally escort to your new home. If you can, visit the home together ahead of time and leave a few small familiar objects behind to help build continuity.

2. Draw a floor plan of the new home and cut out paper furniture so the children can arrange their rooms.

3. Consider painting your child's new room the same color as the old one and arranging the furniture in the same way as before. We always tried to get our boys' rooms settled first, and their beds were always the first furniture to be reassembled.

4. Ask a friend or relative to send your child a welcoming card or letter to your new address so that it's waiting when you arrive. You could also do this yourself.

By planning ahead, you can help your child avoid moving trauma and make the move a fun adventure for your whole family!

PART FIVE

DISCUSSION STARTERS

IS ANGER A FRIEND OR FOE?

Have you ever said to yourself, "This is the last time I'm ever going to get angry"? Doesn't work does it? Anger is hard to control; too often, it controls us! How can we begin to get a handle on anger? Let's look at this common emotion, anger, and how we can process it and make it work for us. Deciding just not to get angry doesn't work. Instead we need to learn how to process our anger.

Let's look at how we are presently dealing with anger and how we would like to deal with it in the future. Take a couple of minutes and reflect on the following questions. You may want to write down your answers.

The first question is: When do I get angry? What things and circumstances really get to me? Write them down.

The second questions is: How do I feel when I am angry? Do I feel hurt, frustrated, or let down?

Third, what do I do when I am angry? Am I the quiet type who sulks and is silent, or do I throw things, shout, and slam doors?

The last question is: What do I wish I would do when I get angry? Here's a chance to think logically through what you'd like your response to be . . . maybe you want to express your feelings calmly to the other person.

Now here is the most helpful tip. The next time anger appears at your house, think about your desired response, process that anger, and make it work for you!

You'll find that anger rightly responded to can be a friend at your house!

KICK THE DISCOURAGEMENT HABIT

Why not kick the discouragement habit at your house and practice more encouragement? The way to get rid of a bad habit is to replace it with a good one.

Here's a four-point action tip to replace the discouragement habit with the encouragement habit.

1. Talk about the pleasant things in your family and marriage team. Identify areas where you would welcome encouragement and support.

2. Make a list of these encouragement areas. Be sure each person has a copy.

3. Now make a commitment to give one another a couple of encouraging comments each day for the next week. If you're encouraged by the first week's experience, extend it for another week.

4. Remember written encouragement. At our

house everyone likes to get notes saying, "You're special!"

Before you know it, you'll have developed the encouragement habit at your house!

FORGIVENESS EXERCISE

No relationship can continue without forgiveness. We don't know what it's like in your family, but in ours there are seven words we have to say often. They are, "I'm sorry. Will you please forgive me?"

These words keep us communicating and help us avoid turning each other off. Let's take a closer look at forgiveness.

Children at a young age can learn the "forgiveness game." Here's how to begin:

Have each family member take turns finishing the sentence, "Forgiveness is . . ." You might say, "Forgiveness is not reminding you that the orange juice was left out again and spoiled." Or, "Forgiveness is giving your dog a juicy bone just after he bites you."

Encourage your kids to put their imaginations to work and see what they come up with. Then look up and read together Jesus's parable in Matthew 18:21-36 about the unforgiving servant.

Take time to forgive one another. It's vital to
your family's health!

TAKING A
YEARLY INVENTORY

In thinking back over the last twelve months, what are you most thankful for?

Too often when we do an evaluation we focus on what we didn't get completed and how tired we are. Unmet expectations can cause disappointment and discouragement.

Here's an exercise we do to help us keep the right focus and verbalize all those things for which we are thankful. You may want to use it in your family.

Give each person a sheet of paper and pencil. Now think back over this last year and list:

1. Three things I'm thankful for. Was your family in good health? Then write it down! You can include any categories you choose like:

   • Things I've seen
   • Things I've learned
   • Things I've done

- Things I've begun
- Things I've finished
- Things I've decided
- Things I've experienced

2. Follow up with this question: "What are you looking forward to in the new year?"

Try it—you'll find it can be a thought-provoking exercise that will help you experience a thankful family.

GENERATION GAP PREVENTER

Have you ever heard this statement, "But Dad, Mom, you grew up in another world!" There's probably some truth in this statement. It is a different world today. But we can use that to build communication in our families. Let's look at some ways we can improve communication and understanding across the generations.

That may sound like mission impossible to you, especially if you have a turtle, but it's really not. What's a turtle? That's the kid who lives in his shell and seldom pokes his neck out to voice his opinion. Of our three sons, we have two talkers and one turtle. But be encouraged—our turtle started talking at age sixteen and was a top debater in college.

Here's a practical suggestion you can use at dinner tonight to get your turtles talking. Why not challenge the kids to list twenty things that were not yet invented when you were their age. Here are a few things you might start with: computers, waterbeds, trash compactors, polyester, and space shuttles.

You may be surprised at all the things you come up with. It may make you feel old! Ask which ones are the most helpful and if we would be better off without some of them.

To cap off the conversation, thank God for all the good things you enjoy as a family in today's world. Not only will your communication be expanded, but the generation gap with your turtles just may disappear!

PREVENTING *FOOT-IN-MOUTH* DISEASE

Do you suffer from foot-in-mouth disease? We're afraid that from time to time, we do. It's difficult to learn when to be quiet. It takes a lot of work. The tongue is in a very slippery place, and it's easy to let unkind words slip out.

Someone said, "The difference between a successful family and a mediocre one consists of leaving about three or four things a day unsaid!" But that is so difficult! Why are we most unkind to those we love the most? Sometimes we're kinder to strangers than we are to those in our home.

Would you say the same things and use the same tone of voice with your best friend or boss that you do with your family? Would you ever walk into your boss' office and tell him that his tie just doesn't go with his suit? Or would you tell a friend his or her apartment looks like a pigpen or ask, "What is growing in the kitchen sink?"

One mother said to her four preschoolers when they all were arguing, "Children, don't you know the Bible says to be kind to one another?" Looking around the room the eldest child said, "It's Ok, Mommy; only the family is here."

What is it like at your house when "only the family" is there? For the next twenty-four hours listen to the conversations in your home. Pretend you're the guest, and notice what you hear. It may be revealing.

If you want to avoid the foot-in-mouth disease, here's a tip. Treat your guests as family and your family as guests.

Remember, it's better to have callouses on our tongues than to suffer from foot-in-mouth disease!

COMMUNICATION KILLERS

Do you have communication killers at your house? In a recent survey conducted at Michigan State University, 79 percent of the parents interviewed said they were communicating with their teenagers, but 81 percent of the teenagers said their parents were not communicating with them.

During the teen years it's not always easy to communicate. There are lots of areas of tension, like friends, money, dress, and schoolwork, to name just a few. To improve communication in these areas, here are some killers you need to avoid:

- First is the classic put-down, like "You can't do anything right" or "You don't know anything about that." Hearing these put-downs, the teen will withdraw from future conversations.

- Another killer is the higher-volume solution. As one person seeks to make his point stronger, he increases the volume. The other person must counter with even higher volume until both parties end up screaming at each other. The next time you get into a volume contest, try lowering your voice while the other continues the loud volume. It can be quite effective.

- Another communication stopper is verbal overkill. Many parents make a statement to their teenager and then restate their position over and over again. Most teens have pretty good hearing, but can be trained to respond only after the fifth or six time. A better approach would be to make sure our teen hears, state the consequences that will occur if he fails to respond, and then be quiet.

Communicating with teens or anyone is hard work, but it will be a lot easier if you can eliminate the communication killers at your house.

MESSY-ROOM EXPERIMENT

Are messy rooms getting you down? Here's an experiment we found helpful to combat the messy-room syndrome. It helped one of our sons to turn his room around—from a disaster area to almost neat.

It takes three weeks to make a new habit, so rather than taking the neatness-for-life approach, we challenged Jonathan to keep his room neat and tidy for twenty-one days. To add motivation, we offered him a dollar a day for twenty-one days.

There were stipulations—no dirty clothes stuffed back in drawers, behind the door, or under the bed. Also the room had to be neat for twenty-one consecutive days. If he missed a day, he had to start counting days all over again.

The results? Twenty-one wonderful, nag-free days and some new tendencies toward neatness. We haven't reached perfection yet, and it's about time to do another twenty-one-day experiment, but we did make some progress in a touchy area without having to nag.

It gave us some feelings of success without making rooms a major issue at our house. Why not give it a try with your Miss Piggy?

DEALING WITH CRISES
IN A POSITIVE WAY

Crises confront every family, and while no one enjoys a crisis, strong families are able to deal with crises in a constructive way. Here's some good news. If we really try, we can see some positive elements in even the darkest of situations.

To help in your home we have some pre-crisis tips for you.

1. Before the next crisis, decide now how you will respond. We'd like to suggest that you take a deep breath and count silently to ten before you say anything. Too often we speak before we think and later regret it. If you do overreact, admit it. During a recent crisis, Claudia realized she was overreacting, so she said, "I know I'm overreacting, but somewhere between this reaction and no reaction is the right reaction!"

2. When you're in a difficult situation ask yourself, "What's the worst thing that could happen,

and what is good about that?" This has really helped us to deal with fears and to see things in perspective.

3. Never, but never, attack family members. Remember, you are a team, and together you will work things out. If you don't attack your family, then together you can attack the problem.

4. Last, look for the humor in the situation. Learn to laugh together when things get tough.

Crises cause strong families to pull together rather than to be pulled apart—as they learn to trust and rely on each other.

PART SIX

MINI-MOMENTS

AFFIRMATION AMMUNITION

Would you say the following statement is true or false? "In a healthy family, the positive and good things about family members are obvious and do not need regular attention."

False! False! False! All of us need to be told often that we are appreciated and why we are! Let's look at some ways to show appreciation. Here are some things you can try.

Why not give your family a shot of affirmation ammunition tonight at dinner? This does assume you're eating together! Take turns telling each family member one thing about him or her that is appreciated.

We recently did this with a group of families at a family conference. One mom's comments expressed well the power of affirmation ammunition: "It sounded so strange to hear positive words come out of my mouth to describe my teenage daughter. . . . But as I said them, they became reality in our relationship."

Maybe you could proclaim Tuesday night as Family Appreciation Night. Let everyone write appreciative comments on a piece of paper. Put the comments in a box, draw them out, and read them. Next week, make the game a mystery game: Leave off the names and guess who's so fantastic.

Don't be guilty of shooting your own troops with cutting and derogatory remarks! There are enough people out there who will tear us down. Our families need all the affirmation we can give them.

As our son Jarrett said, "Home is where you prepare for the battle—not fight it!" Give your family affirmation ammunition today. This is one battle you can win!

FAMILY APPRECIATION

The need to be appreciated is one of the most basic human needs, and one place we can meet this need is in our families. Research shows that one of the most important qualities found in strong families is that family members consistently show appreciation for each other. Let's think about some ways we can do just that.

It's so easy to look at the negative, but for today, we're suggesting that we refocus on the positive and leave lectures and criticism for the family dog.

Here's what we want you to do. Throughout the day as you think of things to tell your mate and children, write them down in short notes like, "You looked great in your new dress today!" or "Thanks for mowing the yard." Then leave the notes around for your loved ones to find.

Many of the things we'd like to tell our loved ones slip by unsaid unless we write them down. And when we write them down, the recipient can go back and reread them.

For a change of pace sometime, why not buy a sack of balloons, inflate them, and write funny or appreciative messages to your family members on them. Then hang, hide, or stuff them all over the house.

Use our suggestions, or come up with your own. But whatever you do, do something today that says to those you love, "I love you—you are appreciated." Your family will be stronger for it!

FEELING INCLUDED

Does everyone in your family feel included? If the answer is, "No" or "I'm not sure," what can you do to promote family unity? It's really important to feel wanted, needed, and included, especially within your own family. Nothing hurts quite like feeling lonesome.

To help you avoid lonesome feelings at your house, here are some tips:

1. Make frequent use of expressions like "It just wouldn't be the same around here without you."

2. Look for the little ways to make someone feel special. Notes and phone calls can really mean a lot. Why not write a short letter expressing how much you appreciate your mate and/or children.

3. Try asking family members for their opinions. We all like to share our thoughts. Dinner time is a great time to draw out other members of the family.

4. Keep memories alive through scrapbooks, slides, home videos, and pictures. Maybe tonight would be a good time to pull out the home movies and look back at your family history. Phrases like "do you remember when . . ." can help create family closeness. Recently when our boys were home for a college break and Jarrett had brought his girlfriend, one of the first things they wanted to do was to pull out the slides of our family. It was fun for us to listen to the boys telling Laurie our family history.

5. Last, don't assume that members of your family know you love them. Tell them—often! Remember, love is the glue that keeps families together.

TEENAGE DRIVERS

A pedestrian is a person who has two cars, a mate, and one or more teenagers. Have you reached that stage of life when you have more drivers in the family than cars? We remember telling Jarrett, by faith, "We're looking forward to your learning to drive. It'll be a great help to us, and we believe you'll be an excellent driver!" He lived up to our expectations. Along the way we found lots of focused time as we each spent hours in the car as supervisor.

We found that if we relaxed and did not fuss too much about the music, we usually had a good time. Goethe, the German philosopher, said, "If we treat a man as he is, he'll stay as he is, but if we treat him as if he were the bigger and better person he can become, he'll become that bigger and better person." Taking Goethe's advice really helps when your teen learns to drive.

You might want to develop your own driving contract with your teen. It could include areas like the number of people allowed in the car, the driving distance allowed, and who pays for insurance. You can decide whether grades will be a factor in driving privileges.

If you have fewer cars than drivers, you have an opportunity to negotiate and work together. Like other stages of life, the learning-to-drive stage can be a growing one. Besides, it's sort of nice to be chauffeured once in a while—or even to walk!

"I DON'T HAVE TIME!"

Does the time factor get in the way of doing things with or for your family? There are exceptions, of course, but generally speaking, we do have the time if we'll just take it.

There's one statement that no one likes to hear: "I just don't have time." Do these exchanges sound familiar? "Honey, can you take a minute and fix this for me?" "Sorry but I don't have the time!" Or the daughter says, "Mom, can you give me a little help with my homework?" Mom's reply? "Can't you see I'm busy!"

Here's an action point for you. The next time you're about to say "I don't have time," in your mind substitute "love" for "time." It may change your priorities around.

Sometimes we're just too inflexible. There are those legitimate times when we have to say, "I can't right now." But many times we could find the time if we would just take it.

Perhaps you are a structured, goal-oriented person. If so, you'll have to work extra hard at being flexible, especially with a family member who throws in a request that draws on your daily time bank.

We need to learn how to put down that project and take advantage of the moments. Remember, moments are all we have. How are you using yours?

Here's our advice: Take the time today to find the time for those you love. You'll all benefit!

TWELVE WORDS CAN CHANGE YOUR HOME

There are twelve words that can change your home, says author Warren Wiersbe. Here are the words that changed his family: "We tried to teach our kids twelve words, not by lecturing them, but by using these ourselves frequently and unconsciously. The first three words are 'please' and 'thank you.'"

Just these three words can change the home atmosphere. Someone gave this advice. Treat your guests as family, and treat your family as guests. Certainly using "please" and "thank you" often will help.

The next two words are "I'm sorry." It's hard for parents to say, but if children hear us say it often to each other and to them, they'll catch on that we're human. They'll learn to say them too. That's certainly how our boys learned to apologize—by watching us!

The next three words are "I love you." These words can never be overused.

The last five words are "I am praying for you." Dr. Wiersbe adds, "Our children knew we prayed for them. And they prayed for us as we shared prayer requests with them."

Maybe these twelve words, "please," "thank you," "I'm sorry," "I love you," and "I'm praying for you," will help to change things for the better at your house. You'll never know until you give them a try!

FIFTY

WHAT IS A FAMILY?

That's not an easy question to answer. Just how would you describe a family? Marriage and family counselor Manny Feldman came up with this definition:

A family is a deeply rooted tree with branches of different strengths, all receiving nourishment from an infinite source.

A family is where character is formed, values are learned, ethics are created, and society is preserved.

A family is where all members contribute and share, cooperate and work, and accept their responsibilities toward the good of the group.

A family is where holidays are celebrated with feasting, birthdays acknowledged with gifts, and thoughts of days gone by, kept alive with fond remembrances.

A family is where each can find solace and comfort in grief, pleasure and laughter in joy, and kindness and encouragement in daily living.

Last she says . . .

A family is a haven of rest, a sanctuary of peace, and most of all, a harbor of love.

To Manny Feldman's definition we'd add that a family is where you can blow it, forget to take out the trash, and still be loved. Brothers and sisters can argue and still be friends. All can be less than perfect and still stick together.

It's great to aim high in our goals as a family, but remember that the bad comes with the good. Here's one last Arp definition: A family is where they still love you, warts and all!

DO YOU HAVE A TURTLE AT YOUR HOUSE?

A turtle is the family member who lives in the clutter he calls a room and comes out three times a day to eat and grunt at the family. How can we draw out the one who usually lives in his shell and occasionally pokes his head out?

Why not try some ten-minute chats? Perhaps bedtime would be a good time to try them. The silent types will often talk just to delay bedtime a few minutes.

Here are some topics to get you started:

1. The funniest person I've ever met . . .

2. Odd places I've fallen asleep . . . (Once Jonathan fell asleep on top of our luggage in the middle of the airport.)

3. A faraway place where I'd like to wake up . . .

4. If I had a million dollars, I'd . . .

5. What I can do best is . . .

6.   My favorite answered prayer . . .

7.   My most embarrassing moment . . .

8.   What I like about our family . . .

It may take longer to tuck your child in bed. But you just may find your turtle is willing to stick his neck out and communicate. See if it works at your house.

SEASONAL SPECIALS

STRESS MONTHS

Did you realize that stress levels soar at different times of the year? September, January, and June are three of those times. What's so stressful about those months?

September is usually a month of change. Kids return to school, but it's to a new grade, class, and teacher.

January is especially stressful because that's when folks try to recover from Christmas and the holidays. That can also include financial stress for generous overspenders.

The other stressful month is June. Again, it's a time of change with kids getting out of school. The least stressful months are March, November, and December.

Perhaps today is a stress time for you. If so, why not do something fun to reduce stress in your home? Perhaps you could surprise your family with their favorite frozen yogurt. Or take your mate some flowers, or share a favorite joke.

Look around you and be creative—you can be a stress reliever in your home.

THE HALLOWEEN SYNDROME

Do you know anyone suffering from the Halloween Syndrome? It's the name given to the stressful, depressed time that many college students experience around the end of October. College freshmen all over the country are candidates for this condition. They face problems and pressures never encountered before as they make the transition from home life to campus life. Thanksgiving is still a month away, and they may be suffering from pangs of homesickness. If you have a college freshman in your family or friendship circle, you can do some things to help cheer them up.

- Write and call more frequently. Encourage your child to call you when he or she feels the need. Our college students feel free to call, and we have the phone bills to prove it.

- Make a brief visit to the campus if possible. Lots of colleges have parents' weekends. But remember, you are on their turf now. Don't crowd your college student with too much parental concern and questioning. We know! We well remember the first time we visited Jarrett. The more we pressed him, the more he retreated. The whole weekend was a disaster, but we're quick learners. Our first college visit to Joel went much more smoothly because we remembered to give him plenty of space.

- Send a surprise care package of your teen's favorite snacks. Sending your college student's favorite brownies just may give you some brownie points.

- Pray for your college student to meet new friends, discover new interests, and find new channels of service.

The Halloween Syndrome doesn't have to be terminal. You can make a difference, so do something today to cheer up a college student you know!

THANKFUL FAMILIES

At this holiday season do you have a thankful family? With all the hustle and bustle of getting ready for the holidays, we want to remind you to take a few moments to focus on your family and say "Thank you" for all the positive things that you see.

You may be thinking, I should be thankful? You just don't know what I'm facing right now. We may be having hard times, but are they worse than what the Pilgrims faced that first Thanksgiving? Over half of their community had died from sickness in that first year, yet they were able to give thanks to God and initiate our Thanksgiving Day.

Just what is thanksgiving? Well, first, it's remembering the things that God has done for us. Why not take a couple of minutes right now to list some of the things that God has done for you and your family?

Second, thanksgiving benefits us. Giving thanks gives us a healthy attitude toward life in general. When we praise and give thanks to God, we are drawn closer to Him. It's hard to be thankful and depressed at the same time.

Last, thanksgiving is a choice. The Pilgrims had a choice: They could have decided to grumble about their hard first year and all the things that went wrong. Instead they chose to give thanks to God; in so doing, they passed down the tradition of thanksgiving to us.

Let us leave you with this thought. The Thanksgiving holiday is well established—but are thankful hearts a vital part of the Thanksgiving tradition at your house? Think about it!

FIFTY FIVE

BIRTHDAY PARTY
FOR JESUS

Are you making Jesus a part of Christmas this year? It's His birthday. One tradition we started when our boys were small was having a birthday party for Jesus—complete with cake and candles.

We chose a coconut cake because this is our favorite. Claudia baked the cake, and Dave grated the fresh coconut. The whole family sang "Happy Birthday," and the boys blew out the candles.

We always have our birthday celebration on Christmas Eve and include a special meal with our favorite foods—like beef fondue. (We keep it simple, but elegant!) Before having the cake, we read the Christmas story from the Gospel of Luke and present our gifts to Jesus.

We top off our birthday celebration by attending a midnight candlelighting service at our church. Christmas Day is family gift-giving time, but our gifts come after we emphasize the real meaning of Christmas on Christmas Eve.

Why not take a few minutes with your family and plan your own birthday party for Jesus? Children love to be involved.

For more good suggestions for building your Christmas celebration around Christ, see *The Christmas Book* (Crossway Books). With a little effort and planning, you'll ensure that Jesus will be the welcomed and honored guest at your home on His birthday!

STORYBOOK CHRISTMASES

Storybook Christmases are reserved for the pages of storybooks! What are your expectations for this holiday season? Are you expecting perfection? If so, then you'll probably be disappointed!

One therapist put it this way: "Too many people have a picture of what the holidays should be like and then feel let down when they don't turn out that way." His advice is, "Don't build up a false image of what's going to happen, be prepared to have some joy and some disappointment." One key to happy and meaningful holidays is to figure out what's important and then do it.

First, list your holiday activities; then organize and set priorities. The experts tell us to be more choosy, not to spin our wheels on little things that don't matter. Then say yes to the important and no to other things. You'll like being in the driver's seat, and your holidays will be more meaningful.

Team up with your family. Doing chores together as a family can cement your relationships and make you feel positive about each other. Here's another tip: Don't expect a relationship to work in December if it doesn't work the rest of the year. What are you doing today to build your relationships with your mate and children?

Gifts are great to get, but much more important is the time you spend with your family building relationships. We asked one of our sons to tell us his favorite Christmas ever. Interestingly, he chose our simplest Christmas. Also interesting was that he couldn't even remember what his gifts were that year.

Right now is a good time to sit down and evaluate your expectations and upcoming activities for the holidays. You may not have a storybook Christmas, but with a little thought and preparation, it can be a meaningful one!

NEW YEAR'S RESOLUTIONS

Making New Year's resolutions is one thing; keeping them is another! The beginning of the year is the traditional time for making a fresh start. A new year, a new beginning, a new chance to strengthen family relationships!

We would like to challenge you to set some resolutions that will help you love your family better. To help you get started, here are some suggestions:

1. Try to find some way every day in the new year to let members of your family know that you love them.

2. Don't let any member of your family feel left out or not cared for.

3. Remember, each member of your family is an individual. Let all of them be who they are and appreciate them for who they are. Don't try to make them over into the persons you

wish they were. We don't want to produce clones.

4. Help make your home a fun place to be.

5. Try to say things to members of your family that lift them up, not drag them down.

6. Don't fret about the past or worry about the future. Live each day to the fullest as it comes along. We can't do anything about yesterday, and tomorrow is unsure. Today is the day!

So resolve today that this coming year is going to be your family's best one yet. Remember, love is the glue that keeps families together.

OVERCOMING THE WINTER BLAHS

Are the winter blahs getting you down? The holiday excitement is over. The holiday bills are piling up. The weather is sometimes depressing, and pockets are empty. Under the circumstances, it's hard to get excited about winter. How can you overcome the winter blahs?

Winter can be exciting. You don't believe us? Try some of the following suggestions to add some excitement and chase away the blahs:

1. Try a new recipe and have each one at the table share something he or she would like to do in the new year.

2. If you have a fireplace, make a fire in the fireplace and roast hot dogs.

3. Call or write someone you haven't contacted in a long time. Write a note of encourage-

ment to someone you know who's having problems.

4. Bring a picnic lunch to work with a checkered tablecloth, French bread, and cold cuts, and share it with your co-workers. You could even stick in some colored hard-boiled eggs for originality!

5. Window shop with a twist. List all the things you already have that you see in the store windows or mail order catalogs. Most of us have more than we realize. Then thank God for your abundance of blessings.

6. Consider visiting a nursing home or hospital. Many people in these institutions rarely get visitors, especially in January.

7. And in case of snow, be the first to organize a neighborhood snowball fight.

Take our advice. Before you know it, you will have exchanged the winter blahs for winter joys. And remember, spring is just around the corner!

END-OF-SCHOOL BLUES

Does anyone at your house have end-of-school blues? Summer vacation may be fast approaching. School is still in session, but your children are already in the "vacation mode." How can you survive the last days of school?

This is the time of year things get hectic at our house with exams, school programs, sports tournaments, recitals, and graduation activities. What can we do in the midst of busy schedules to encourage our kids to hang in for another few days?

When our boys were younger, they used to love notes of encouragement: "You can do it," "We're praying for you," or "Summer's on the way. . . . Hang in there."

Why not take a few extra minutes and greet your "schooler" with his or her favorite cookies. Anything that says "You're special" or "I understand you're tired of school" seems to be appreciated at our house.

Try it at your house. You may win the popular parent award—or hear those rare words, "Gee, thanks. I appreciate you!"

SANITY IN THE SUMMERTIME

Is it really possible to experience sanity in the summertime? Before we know it summer will be upon us. Too many parents just let the summer happen with insane results. Why not take control this year and make the summer happen?

Sanity in the summertime can happen if we're willing to put forth a little effort and make it happen. The key word is planning. Why not plan a date this week with your mate to sit down and talk about the upcoming summer and begin to make some plans?

To get started, answer these three questions:

1. "What?" What do you want to see happen this summer? For instance, do you want to develop a closer personal relationship with your children? Do you want to work on your communication or on building your child's self-esteem?

You can set your summer's goals based on your answers to the "What?" question. Remember to include something for your marriage—like summer dating or a twenty-four-hour getaway. Also remember that parents need time to grow individually.

2. "How?" This gets down to the practical. What can we do to reach these goals? List possible activities. For instance, to build communication, maybe you'll make finger puppets and use open-ended questions to help your child open up and talk!

3. "When?" Make a tentative schedule for the summer. For instance, maybe every Wednesday will become Children's Day, and you'll set aside that time to do special things with your children. Perhaps Mom and Dad will get a babysitter each Saturday afternoon.

For more ideas, may we refer you to Claudia's book, *Sanity in the Summertime*. And as you plan your summer, you'll find that you too can actually experience summertime sanity!

BIBLIOGRAPHY

Arp, Claudia. *Beating the Winter Blues.* Nashville, TN: Thomas Nelson Publishers, 1991.

Arp, Claudia, and Linda Dillow. *Sanity in the Summertime.* Nashville, TN: Thomas Nelson Publishers, 1981.

Arp, Dave, and Claudia Arp. *52 Dates for You and Your Mate.* Nashville, TN: Thomas Nelson Publishers, 1983.

Arp, Dave, and Claudia Arp. *The Marriage Track.* Nashville, TN: Thomas Nelson Publishers, 1992.

Campbell, Ross. *How to Really Love Your Child.* Wheaton, IL: Tyndale House Publishers, 1982.

Dobson, James. *The Strong-Willed Child.* Wheaton, IL: Tyndale House Publishers, 1988.

Kesler, Jay. *Parents and Teenagers.* Wheaton, IL: Victor Books, 1984.

King, Pat. *How to Have All the Time You Need Every Day.* Wheaton, IL: Tyndale House Publishers, 1980.

Liontos, Lynn, and Demetri Liontos. *The Good Couple Life.* Winston-Salem, NC: The Association of Couples in Marriage Enrichment, Inc., 1982.

McGinnis, Alan Loy. *The Friendship Factor.* Minneapolis, MN: Augsburg Publishing House, 1979.

Mace, David. *Close Companions: The Marriage Enhancement Handbook.* New York: Continuum, 1982.

Mace, David, and Vera Mace. *How to Have a Happy Marriage.* Nashville, TN: Abingdon Press, 1977.

_____. *Love and Anger in Marriage*. Grand Rapids, MI: Zondervan Publishing House, 1982.

Peterson, J. Alan. *The Marriage Affair*. Wheaton, IL: Tyndale House Publishers, 1974.

Ridenour, Fritz. *What Teenagers Wish Their Parents Knew About Kids*. Waco, TX: Word Publishers, 1982.

Sell, Charles. *Achieving the Impossible: Intimate Marriage*. New York: Ballentine, 1982.

Stanley, Phyllis, and Miltinnie Yih. *Celebrate the Seasons*. Colorado Springs, CO: Nav Press, 1986.

COLOPHON

The typeface for the text of this book is a modern version of *Goudy Old-style*, made more suitable for text typesetting because of a tighter set and a more subtle presentation of the distinctive flourishes that characterize it. Its creator, Frederick W. Goudy, was commissioned by American Type Founders Company to design a new Roman type face. Completed in 1915 and named Goudy Old Style, it was an instant bestseller. However, its designer had sold the design outright to the foundry, so when it became evident that additional versions would be needed to complete the family, the work was done by the foundry's own designer, Morris Benton. From the original design came seven additional weights and variants, all of which sold in great quantity. However, Goudy himself received no additional compensation for them. He later recounted a visit to the foundry with a group of printers, during which the guide stopped at one of the busy casting machines and stated, "Here's where Goudy goes down to posterity, while American Type Founders goes down to prosperity." The perfect blend of beauty and versatility of this classic and graceful design adds distinction wherever it's used. It is considered the most popular advertising typeface in use today.

A B O U T   T H E   A U T H O R S

For more than fifteen years, Dave and Claudia Arp have conducted marriage and family enrichment workshops and are co-founders of Marriage Alive International. They have authored or co-authored several books, including *52 Dates for You and Your Mate*, *The Marriage Track*, *Beating the Winter Blues*, and *Sanity in the Summertime* (co-authored with Linda Dillow).

Dave and Claudia have three sons and live in Knoxville, Tennessee.